EUROPA ⚔ MILITARIA Nº21

THE
ROYAL MARINES

IN THE '90s

Andy Evans

Windrow & Greene

Dedication: This book is dedicated to my dear parents Allan and Violet Evans, for their everlasting love and support

Designed by Frank Ainscough
Printed in Great Britain by
Amadeus Press Ltd, Huddersfield

This edition published in
Great Britain 1997 by
Windrow & Greene Ltd.
5 Gerrard Street
London W1V 7LJ

A CIP catalogue record for this book is available from the British Library

ISBN 1 85915 072 1

Acknowledgements:
To individually thank everyone involved in the production of this book would probably double the page count, but special mention must be made of the following: Capt.John Glaze, Royal Marines Public Relations Officer at Ministry of Defence, London; Dick Stokes, RMPR0 at the Commando Training Centre, Lympstone; all the RMPR staff at Portsmouth, and Matthew Little at the Royal Marines Museum; 3 Commando Brigade Media Team; and all the individual units and men - you know who you are. . . Thanks are also due to Robin Adshead, Tony Simpson, Patrick Allen; David Reynolds of Photo Press Defence Pictures, Plymouth; Peter Russell and the Military Picture Library, Aldershot; and of course to Martin Windrow, for his support and patience with the project. The editor also wishes to acknowledge his debt to the published work of Nick van der Byl, Brien Hobbs and Will Fowler.

INTRODUCTION

Amongst the specialised units of the world's fighting forces the British Royal Marine Commandos stand acclaimed as an elite by their contemporaries. Modest in numbers, the Corps is recognised internationally as standing in the front rank by virtue of their very high levels of individual commitment, of operational versatility, and of military skills.

The Royal Marines trace their history to the Duke of York and Albany's Maritime Regiment, raised in October 1664 "to be in readiness to be distributed in His Majesty's Fleet prepared for sea service". As an island nation whose expanding wealth and influence depended entirely upon maritime activity, Britain was involved over the next 250 years in countless combined operations on foreign shores. The Royal Marines played a major role in these greatest years of the Royal Navy, serving as small arms marksmen and boarding parties in ship actions, as the backbone of landing parties for shore action, as ceremonial guards (and the ultimate guarantors of shipboard discipline), and later as gun turret crews on major warships.

Among the military assumptions called brutally into question by the significant advances in technology and scale of operations during the First World War was the practicality of major troop landings on enemy-defended shores; the Gallipoli campaign, by far the largest such operation so far seen, ended in costly failure. At the outset of the Second World War the Corps was serving in its traditional role, providing ships' detachments; but the participation of Royal Marines alongside Army units in

the new Commando raiding forces from 1942 showed the way forward. By 1943-44 three Special Service Brigades had evolved to spearhead major landings in Italy, North-West Europe and the Far East, one formed entirely from RM Commandos and the others of mixed RM and Army composition; and the disbandment of Army Commandos in 1946 left the Royal Marines the sole inheritors of the Commando tradition.

Following the end of conscription in Britain in 1959 the Royal Marines became an entirely Commando-trained force. During Britain's slow retreat from Empire in the 1950s-60s the Corps fought in the Middle East and Far East, developing new techniques such as helicopter insertion from dedicated "Commando carriers". Today's Royal Marines have a distinctive strategic role; alongside nuclear submarines and carrier-based air power, the Corps' amphibious and airmobile warfare skills provide one of the three core capabilities of the Royal Navy. This strategic role requires them to be familiar with operations in all types of terrain, from European to jungle, desert, and arctic warfare; and to be trained for delivery to battle either by helicopter, by landing craft or by small, high-speed boat.

The stunning collapse of the Soviet Union in the early 1990s destroyed the relative certainties of the fifty-year Cold War, facing defence planners with an unstable and unpredictable world. The new emphasis on highly flexible and mobile forces capable of rapid intervention in a variety of environments, projecting fighting power ashore independent of shore-based infrastructure, underlines the special value of the Royal Marines as a key strategic asset.

THE ROYAL MARINES SINCE WORLD WAR II

The Normandy landings of 6 June 1944 and the subsequent operations - the greatest combined operation in history - involved some 17,000 Royal Marines. The mixed 1st Special Service Bde. including 45 RM Cdo. formed the extreme eastern flank of the seaborne invasion force, advancing from Sword Beach to link up with 6th Airborne Division on the River Orne. The all-RM 4th Special Service Bde. (41, 46, 47 & 48 RM Cdos.) fought at the junction of Sword and Juno Beaches and on Gold Beach. Both brigades were heavily engaged until September in the bocage fighting and the break-out which followed. The 4th SS Bde. subsequently fought at Walcheren, and 1st Bde. joined them on the Maas during the punishing winter fighting before spearheading the Rhine crossings in March 1945. (From December 1944 the formations were retitled Commando Brigades, the former abbreviation "SS" having unfortunate associations in 1944-45).

RM Commandos had already seen considerable action in the Mediterranean, 2, 3, 40 RM & 41 RM Cdos. fighting in Sicily and at Salerno and Termoli in Italy in June-October 1943. In October the 2nd SS Bde. was formed (2, 9, 40 RM & 43 RM Cdos., & 10 Inter-Allied Cdo.), and units of this formation fought at Anzio, in the Dalmatian Islands, in Yugoslavia and in Italy. Nos.42 RM and 44 RM Cdos. fought the Japanese with 3rd Special Service/Commando Bde. in the Arakan and Burma.

The Early Post-War Years

Despite the inevitable massive reduction in forces which followed the war the Royal Marines retained the Commando mission, the green beret (which originated with No.1 Army Cdo. in 1942), and the 3rd Cdo.Bde. formation comprising 40, 42 and 45 RM Commandos. The brigade saw service in Palestine in 1946-47; in Hong Kong in 1949; and from 1950 against Communist guerrillas in Perak during the Malayan Emergency. That same year 41 Cdo. was reformed and deployed to Korea, fighting under US 1st Marine Division in the terrible Chosin retreat and winning a US Presidential Unit Citation. In 1951 the unit carried out coastal operations behind North Korean lines; and was disbanded on return to England in 1952.

In 1955-59 the EOKA rising on Cyprus took 3 Cdo.Bde. to that island. This campaign was interrupted by the Anglo-French Suez operation of November 1956; 40 and 42 Cdos. carried out amphibious landings, and at Port Said some 400 men of 45 Cdo. made the world's first assault deployment of infantry by helicopter, flying from carriers several miles offshore. One of the lessons of Suez was Britain's overall weakness in capacity to project power overseas, however, and a major consequence was the conversion at the beginning of the 1960s of the first of three aircraft carriers, HMS *Bulwark*, into a Commando carrier - Landing Platform Helicopter (LPH), in naval jargon - capable of accomodating and lifting an expanded Commando. Nos. 41 and 43 Cdos. were reformed in 1960-61.

Commandos waiting to move inland from the Normandy beaches, on 6 June 1944. (Royal Marines Museum)

The 1960s and 1970s

During the 1960s 42 Cdo. was based at Singapore, 40 Cdo. later following them there from Malta, and 45 Cdo. at Aden. Army Commandos reappeared in 1962-63 with the conversion of 29 & 95 Regts.RA to the Commando artillery role, followed by three Air Troops in support, and subsequently by Commando Engineer and Commando Brigade Air Squadrons. In 1961 HMS *Bulwark* helicoptered 42 Cdo. ashore in Kuwait to deter a threatened Iraqi invasion, followed by 45 Cdo. from Aden. That flyblown but strategic corner of Arabia was itself torn by unrest during the mid-1960s, and 42 and 45 Cdos. saw service there. Trouble also broke out in the Far East in 1962 when Indonesia threatened the Borneo territories of newly independent Malaysia. HQ 3 Cdo.Bde. arrived in December, and until 1966 40 and 42 Cdos. saw considerable service in challenging jungle, coastal and riverine operations.

The 1968 Defence White Paper foreshadowed the complete withdrawal of permanent British garrisons from the Far and Middle East. The Royal Marines' strategic focus now shifted to NATO's Allied Forces Northern Europe (AFNORTH), beginning the Commandos' still current special emphasis on arctic warfare on NATO's northern flank in Norway. The disbandment of 43 Cdo. and 95 Cdo.Regt.RA brought total strength down to about 8,000. The LPHs were replaced by two amphibious assault ships (Landing Platforms Dock, LPD), HMS *Fearless* and *Intrepid*.

As a background to their operations further afield, since the outbreak of disorder in Northern Ireland in 1969 the individual Commando units have frequently served their turn in the province on four- or six- month tours of duty, carrying out every kind of security mission from urban and border patrols to small boat work. In 1981, 41 Cdo. was once more disbanded.

The Falklands and the Gulf

On 2 April 1982 the military junta then ruling the Argentine launched an invasion of the Falkland Islands in the South Atlantic - a sparsely-inhabited British possession long claimed by Argentina - in order to distract their restless population with a patriotic adventure. Platoon-sized garrisons of Royal Marines on South Georgia and East Falkland islands were overwhelmed. In Britain 3 Cdo.Bde., under Brig.Julian Thompson, was warned for immediate deployment over 8,000 miles south to one of the most remote and inhospitable spots on earth. By 17 April the Amphibious Task Force had assembled at Ascension Island in the South Atlantic.

On 25 April elements of 42 Cdo. retook South Georgia; and on 21 May 3 Cdo.Bde. - with 40, 42 and 45 Cdo. and other brigade assets, plus 2nd and 3rd Bns. The Parachute Regt. under command - landed at San Carlos Water in the north-west of East Falkland and successfully established a beachhead and logistic base, despite fierce Argentine air attacks. At the beginning of June a second formation landed: 5 Inf.Bde., with two Guards battalions and one of Gurkha Rifles. This allowed formation of Land Forces Falkland Islands, commanded by Maj.Gen.Jeremy Moore RM. On 31 May both brigades broke out of the beachhead, heading for the main Argentine positions around Port Stanley in the east; 3 Cdo.Bde. took a punishing northerly route across the island, with 42 Cdo. seizing Mts.Kent and Challenger. Initially 40 Cdo. guarded the base area, but two companies later operated at Mt.Harriet, which was taken by 42 Cdo.; 45 Cdo.

One of the most famous images of the 1982 Falklands War: 45 Commando's infamous "yomp" across the miserable winter terrain of East Falkland towards Stanley, almost entirely without mechanical transport, was a feat of old-fashioned infantry soldiering which the enemy had not imagined possible. (RM Museum)

captured Two Sisters mountain. With the loss of their well-prepared hill positions outside Stanley the large Argentine forces on the island surrendered on 14 June.

Following the Falklands War, in which the success of British forces was the more impressive given the extreme challenge that it represented to only barely adequate resources, strategists re-examined the whole question of Out of Area Operations. A tri-service Joint Force Headquarters was formed to handle such operations, for which the principle combat assets were planned to be 3 Commando and 5 Airborne Brigades.

These forces were not committed to Operation Granby, the deployment of British forces to the Arabian Gulf as part of the Coalition formed to reverse Iraq's invasion of Kuwait in 1990-91; but although the liberation of Kuwait was a task for heavy armoured units, individual personnel and small specialist parties served ashore and aboard Royal Navy and Royal Fleet Auxiliary vessels during the campaign.

The subsequent Operation Haven between April and July 1991 saw 3 Cdo.Bde. (less 42 Cdo.) deployed to the wild mountains of northern Iraq as part of a multi-national force of some 23,000 men. Their mission was to shelter, feed, heal, and guard in so-called "safe havens" up to half a million Kurdish refugees who had fled from Saddam Hussein's murderous revenge for a Kurdish rising against his regime in the aftermath of the Gulf War. The Royal Marines showed themselves adept and dedicated in this humanitarian role; they also cleared large numbers of mines, and were successful in a number of firefights against probing Iraqi forces.

5

THE ROYAL MARINES IN THE '90s

The Royal Marines Command, an integral part of the Royal Navy, consists of the personnel and units (including Royal Navy, RM Reserve, Army and Royal Air Force) who are the responsibility of the budget (currently some £224 million annually) of the Commandant General Royal Marines. The Royal Marines Command reports to the Commander-in-Chief Fleet. The commander of 3 Commando Brigade is the Garrison Commander of all brigade units; however, the operational command of the Special Boat Squadron is delegated to the Director Special Forces at the Ministry of Defence. Currently there are just under 7,000 trained Royal Marines, with a further 1,220 in the Royal Marines Reserve.

The primary missions of the Royal Marines can be summarised as follows:
(1) To provide a Commando Brigade to plan, mount and sustain all types of amphibious operations; and to conduct land operations as a light brigade.
(2) To provide detachments aboard naval ships and at shore bases.
(3) To provide specialist units - e.g. the Special Boat Squadron and Assault Squadrons.
(4) To conduct operations other than war, and to maintain expertise in mountain and cold weather operations.

(5) To provide rapid reaction forces to protect UK off-shore oil platforms, and for counter-terrorist operations in a maritime environment.
(6) To provide a guard for the UK independent nuclear deterrent.
(7) To provide bands for the Royal Marines and Royal Navy.

(Below) Royal Marines of 40 Cdo. are inspected by a former Commandant General of the Corps, Gen.Robin Ross. All ranks wear the green beret of the trained Commando, with the badge of a wreathed globe surmounted by a lion and crown, and the lovat-green service dress introduced as Royal Marines No.2 dress in 1964. All officers and WO1s wear a navy blue silk lanyard on the left shoulder; officers and men of the three Commandos wear a second lanyard on the right in identifying colours: sky blue, white or red for 40, 42 or 45 Commandos respectively. The captain at left wears dress parachute wings in gold and silver on black on his right upper arm; the sergeant at right, the South Atlantic and General Service campaign medals.

(Right) No.1 dress - "blues", with the white cap - is seldom worn except by bandsmen; this Marine of 45 Cdo. is on duty at Horse Guards Parade, London,

during a ceremonial occasion. The Corps collar badges are uncrowned. His Military General Service Medal bears the Northern Ireland clasp.

(Far right) The officer's No.1 dress blues and white cap worn by a Royal Marines major. The lion and crown of the cap badge (the "dog and basket") is a separate casting for officers, and the globe is silver. This field officer (note gold peak trim) wears on his left arm the King's Badge, showing that he was the best recruit in his troop; and General Service and United Nations medals.

(Below right) Royal Marines bands have an unrivalled reputation for excellence. Their No.1 dress is a much more ornate version of the "blues", worn with a whitened Wolseley helmet. Bandsmen serve as stretcher bearers in time of war. (All photos Photo Press Defence Picture Library, Plymouth)

MAKING A MARINE

The Commando Training Centre Royal Marines is situated at Lympstone, Devon. Commanded by a colonel, the CTCRM has a staff of just over 800 service personnel and about 100 civilians; in all some 2,000 students pass through the centre's five Wings each year. Its task is to provide Regular and Reserve personnel of the Royal Marines with new entry, command, and specialist training; and to provide specialist training for personnel of the Royal Navy, Army and Royal Air Force posted to serve with the Commando Brigade. The CTCRM is unique in that all ranks and specialities train in the same establishment, thus fostering *esprit de corps.*

Each year some 1,100 Royal Marine recruits complete a 30-week basic training course with Commando Training Wing - the longest for infantry soldiers anywhere in the world. The course is extremely demanding; it is designed not only to instil physical fitness and teach military skills, but to promote teamwork, resilience, stamina, and cheerfulness in adversity: "to train a man to take his place with confidence as a rifleman in a Commando, and to ensure that he understands his role as a responsible citizen." Officers' Training Wing receives some 60 young officers annually; joining as second lieutenants, they must complete 14 months of training before appointment to Commandos as troop (i.e. platoon) commanders.

For all ranks the prized green beret of the Commando can only be gained by successfully completing a separate four-week phase of their training regimes, culminating in "test week", when all would-be Commandos must undergo a gruelling series of timed events. These include speed marching in full kit over six-and nine-mile courses, completing an aerial assault course and an endurance course of underground tunnels and waterways, and a four-mile run back to camp. The final test is the "30-miler": map-reading and "yomping" across the treacherous, windswept countryside of Dartmoor, carrying equipment, inside an eight-hour time limit. To quote one RM instructor, "It's a right ball-breaker; you need the stamina of an ox and the sure-footedness of a mountain goat."

The Non-Commissioned Officers' Training Wing provides progressive leadership training for some 400 NCOs per year. Each year Infantry Support Wing provides additional training for about 800 men of all ranks required to operate specialist equipment and weapons, and for RM specialist instructors throughout the naval service; categories include snipers, assault engineers, and physical training, drill and weapons instructors. Signal & Clerk Training Wing trains some 250 personnel yearly in signals, clerical and stores accountancy skills, and about 320 RM and attached personnel in computer and IT skills.

(Left and above) At 30 weeks, the course at the Commando Training Centre, Lympstone, is the longest for infantry soldiers anywhere in the world. Before the phase during which they must qualify for the coveted green beret, recruits ("Noddies") wear the dark blue beret with the RM badge on a red arch-shaped backing.

(Right) Loosing off an 81mm mortar round. Combat dress for the Royals is the standard range of DPM camouflage clothing, and the GS Mk 6 helmet. (All photos CTC Lympstone)

THE CUTTING EDGE – 3 COMMANDO BRIGADE

The landing force for amphibious operations is formed by 3 Commando Brigade; this is reinforced for some NATO deployments by elements of the Royal Netherlands Marine Corps, together forming UK/NL Landing Force. The formation from 1996 of the Joint Rapid Deployment Force (JRDF), as a response to the unpredictable nature of worldwide threats in the aftermath of the Cold War, has intensified the brigade's already high level of co-operation with Royal Navy, Army and Royal Air Force assets. The brigade may be deployed with elements of 3 (UK) Division, with whom they mount regular exercises.

The Commando Brigade is in essence an amphibious light infantry brigade, able to call upon specialist skills, training, weaponry and support. A rigorous cycle of training in scenarios as diverse as mountain and arctic, jungle and desert warfare gives the brigade a "go anywhere" capability; and it packs a punch disproportionate to its size. The steady reductions in the size of Britain's armed forces over the past 30 years have had one beneficial effect: the careful management of limited assets has engendered versatility and flexibility. The unexpected challenge of the Falklands War in 1982 led to a welcome re-examination of the doctrine of Out of Area Operations, from which the amphibious forces have benefited.

The brigade is structured around three Commandos - battalion-sized light infantry units - reinforced by combat support and service support units which provide the specialist skills required by an amphibious force tasked with rapid reaction and sustainable intervention. In time of conflict the brigade would be enhanced by Royal Marine Reservists and Territorial Army Commando gunners, sappers and logistic elements.

The brigade has its own artillery regiment for indirect fire support; an air defence battery and a seperate light air defence troop; and an integral engineer squadron. The Commando Logistics Regiment is responsible for all the essential combat supplies, vehicles and medical support to sustain the force ashore. Also incorporated is an assault squadron with landing craft, hovercraft and light raiding craft which provide waterborne tactical mobility. Two Naval Air Commando Squadrons provide medium lift helicopters to move men, weapons systems and stores; a third

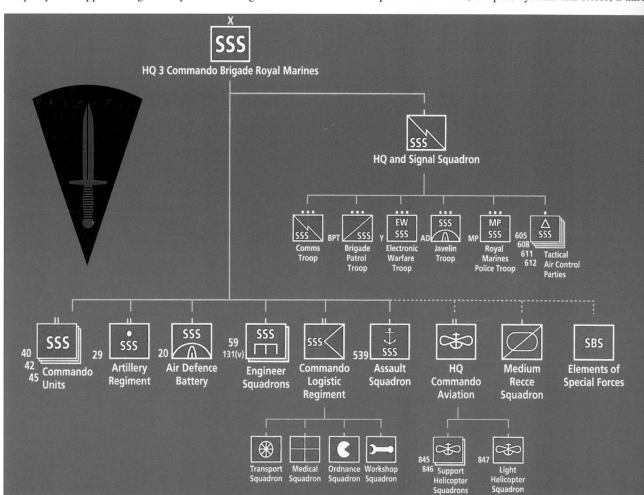

Above & right) As required, a Medium Reconnaissance Squadron for 3 Cdo.Bde. is provided by an Army unit - currently, the CVR(T) Scimitars of B Sqn., The Household Cavalry.

Left) Chart of 3 Cdo.Bde. organisation; broken lines indicate assets attached as required. Not shown is the Royal Netherlands Marine Corps 1st Amphib. Combat Grp. (equivalent to a Commando) which has trained with the RM Cdos.for many years and which would serve with the brigade in time of war under NATO command.

The WWII dagger shoulder flash is an Army rather than a RM badge of Commando service, and is worn today by gunners, sappers and other former 3 Cdo.Bde. personnel after returning to other Army units. (Chart courtesy Royal Marines)

squadron is equipped with TOW-armed light helicopters for anti-tank firepower and others for casevac and reconnaissance. Tactical air control parties are trained to direct the Royal Navy's Sea Harrier and the RAF's Harrier GR.7 V/STOL jet fighter-bombers. The brigade's main assets are as follows:

HQ 3 Commando Brigade, & Signal Squadron

The brigade commander's command and control unit (C2).
Communications Troop Responsible for secure communications and satellite link-ups with the units.
Brigade Patrol Troop Six teams of Mountain Leaders -specialists in mountain, cold weather and cliff assault techniques - provide Brigade HQ with medium range reconnaissance for early warning and intelligence gathering, commonly out to 60km (40 miles) ahead of the brigade.
Y Troop The brigade's electronic warfare specialists.
Air Defence Troop A small, highly mobile detachment armed with Shorts S15 Javelin shoulder-fired guided SAMs, providing point air defence for high value assets.
RM Police Troop Provides close protection to the Brigade Commander as well as co-ordination of vehicle movements from a beachhead, marking of main supply routes and convoy escort.
Tactical Air Control Parties Four TACPs (three Regular, one Reserve) are responsible for directing RN and RAF close air support.

Commando Units

See accompanying diagrams.
40 and 42 Commandos, based respectively at Norton Manor Camp in Somerset and in Plymouth, each have a five-company structure: HQ Coy., with Signals Quartermaster and MT Troops and Medical Section, Support Coy., with Mortar, Anti-tank, and Recce Troops and Assault Engineer Section; and three Rifle Companies.
45 Commando, based at Arbroath, Scotland, is a unique force grouping with additional artillery and logistics elements.

A Commando is equipped with about 70 wheeled vehicles and 30 tracked all-terrain vehicles (ATVs) provide a highly mobile platform for the unit's machine guns, mortars, and MILAN ATGWs. The Commando is able to operate for up to three days as a self-sustaining force using the supplies and ammunition carried on the ATVs and by the men. A planned enhancement of firepower will see an allocation of the venerable but still unrivalled Browning M2 .50cal. heavy machine gun.
29 Commando Regiment Royal Artillery Three Regular and one Volunteer batteries each of 6x 105mm Light Guns, which can be towed by Land Rover or ATV or carried underslung by Sea King helicopters; HQ, Workshops and two Regular batteries based at Plymouth, one Regular with 45 Cdo. at Arbroath, 289 Bty.(V) in London and Bournemouth, and 148 Bty. at Poole, Dorset. The Forward Observation elements, of mixed Royal Artillery and Royal Navy composition, are highly trained in Special Forces techniques.
20 Commando Air Defence Battery Royal Artillery Equipped with Rapier FSB2 SAM system.
59 Independent Commando Squadron Royal Engineers
131 (V) Independent Cdo. Squadron Royal Engineers Both the Regular and Volunteer squadrons provide a Recce Troop and several Field Troops for close sapper support, e.g. bridge building, demolition, mine laying and clearance.
Commando Logistic Regiment Based at Chivenor, Devon, and tasked to provide support for assault units operating from a sea base, and if need be to develop a shore base, ensuring combat resupply. The regiment is 670 strong, 80% RM-manned but

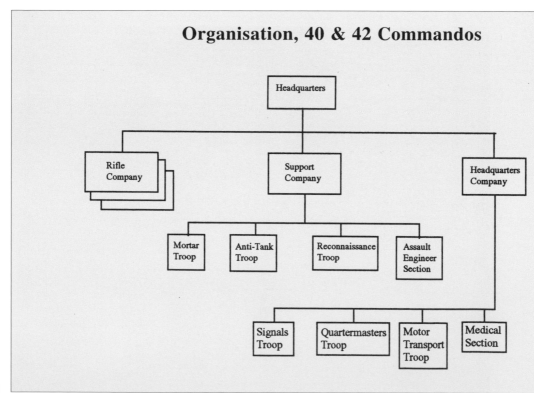

Organisation, 40 & 42 Commandos

Right) The MILAN ATGW, of which 24 are carried by the anti-tank elements of each Commando, giving formidable firepower out to 2,000m.

Below left) The organisation of 40 and 42 Cdos. is identical. Each has 656 all ranks, 9x51mm mortars, 9x 81mm mortars, 24x MILAN ATGW, 100x 94mm shoulder-fired anti-tank weapons, and 13x GP machine guns in the sustained fire role.

Below) The structure of 45 Cdo. is unique, including integral artillery and logistic elements which allow the force increased independence on operations. Its establishment is 795 all ranks.

Organisation, 45 Commando

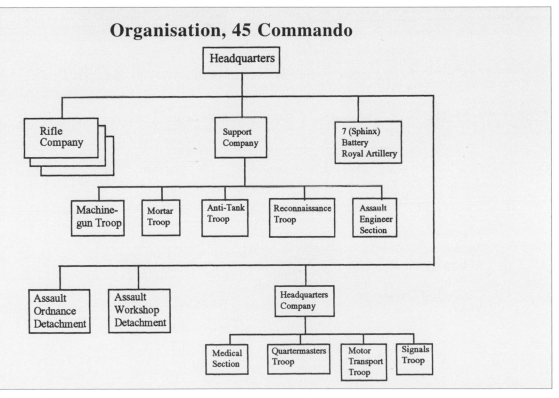

- **Headquarters**
  - **Rifle Company**
  - **Support Company**
    - Machine-gun Troop
    - Mortar Troop
    - Anti-Tank Troop
    - Reconnaissance Troop
    - Assault Engineer Section
    - Assault Ordnance Detachment
    - Assault Workshop Detachment
    - **Headquarters Company**
      - Medical Section
      - Quartermasters Troop
      - Motor Transport Troop
      - Signals Troop
  - **7 (Sphinx) Battery Royal Artillery**

including Royal Navy and Army personnel (RAMC, REME, RLC, AGC, RS), and has some 340 assorted vehicles. Apart from HQ Sqn. it comprises:

Transport Sqn., which moves all the brigade's daily requirements in ammunition, fuel and rations with a wide variety of vehicles including 4- and 14-ton trucks, and prime movers and trailers for the DROPS rapid cargo handling system; *Medical Sqn.*, which provides two dressing stations and an ambulance troop - this has a Royal Navy component, and in wartime is enhanced by RN field surgical teams; *Workshop Sqn.*, which recovers and repairs all brigade equipment - weapons, vehicles, radios, optics, etc.; and *Ordnance Sqn.*, which provides technical and specialist spares support, with responsibility for all ammunition, rations, spares and fuel.

539 Assault Squadron RM Operates Rigid and Inflatable Raiding Craft, hovercraft, and landing craft, and can be used to support pre-assault advance force operations as well as co-operating with 4 and 6 ASRMs based aboard the assault ships (LPDs).

HQ Commando Aviation Co-ordinates the aviation support required by the brigade, with 845 and 846 Naval Air Commando Squadrons (medium lift) and 847 NACS (light and A/T) under command.

Assets which may be assigned to 3 Cdo.Bde. at need also include:

Medium Reconnaissance Squadron An Army element provided by a detached squadron from a Royal Armoured Corps unit, equipped with CVR(T) series light armoured vehicles.

Special Forces Normally from the Special Boat Squadron (see below), assigned to the brigade to conduct advance operations ahead of any main force.

Other Royal Marine Units:

Special Boat Squadron The SBS provides the Royal Navy and Royal Marines with their main Special Forces capability, with emphasis on beach reconnaissance and intelligence gathering,

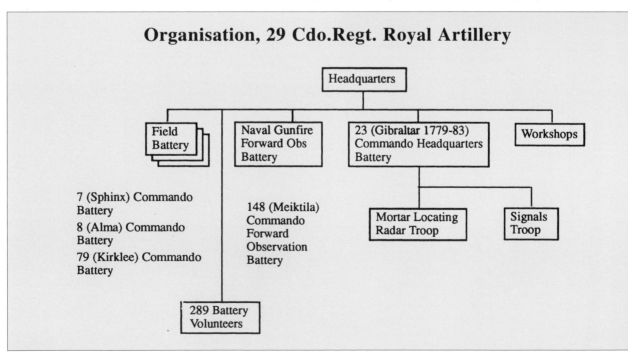

Organisation, 29 Cdo.Regt. Royal Artillery

Headquarters

- Field Battery
- Naval Gunfire Forward Obs Battery
- 23 (Gibraltar 1779-83) Commando Headquarters Battery
- Workshops

7 (Sphinx) Commando Battery
8 (Alma) Commando Battery
79 (Kirklee) Commando Battery

148 (Meiktila) Commando Forward Observation Battery

Mortar Locating Radar Troop

Signals Troop

289 Battery Volunteers

Below left) The brigade's integral artillery is provided by the 600 Commando-trained gunners of 29 Cdo.Regt.Royal Artillery. Each battery has 6x 105mm Light Guns and two or three Forward Observation parties. 289 Bty., a Territorial Army unit, provides an additional gun battery and Naval Gunfire Observation Troop when mobilised. The Mortar Locating Radar Troop is equipped with Cymbeline MLR. The Workshops are a REME recovery and repair unit. On NATO mobilisation 29 Regt. takes under command the 120mm heavy mortars of a Royal Netherlands Marine Corps battery.

Left) Carrying some 65kg (130lbs) of equipment, men of 42 Cdo. land from LCUs on a Hebrides beach during Exercise Iron Maiden.

Right & below) The brigade's Air Defence Troop are equipped with Javelin SAM launchers. (Photos Robin Adshead)

Organisation, Commando Logistic Regiment

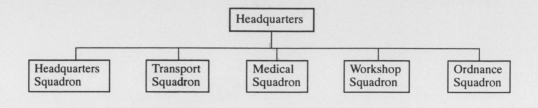

```
                          Headquarters
                               |
   +-----------+-----------+-----------+-----------+
   |           |           |           |           |
Headquarters Transport  Medical    Workshop   Ordnance
Squadron     Squadron   Squadron   Squadron   Squadron
```

Organisation, ATTURM

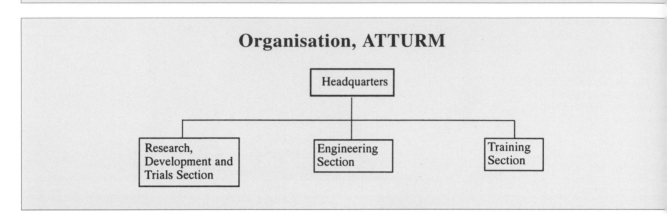

```
                    Headquarters
                         |
   +---------------------+---------------------+
   |                     |                     |
Research,            Engineering           Training
Development and      Section               Section
Trials Section
```

Below left) One of the 'Loggies'' versatile Eager Beaver vehicles disengages the roller unit of the Class 30 trackway which it has just laid across the beach; in the background, a Sea King helicopter lifts ashore one of 29 Regt's 105mm Light Guns.

Right) A 4-ton 4x4 truck of the Cdo.Log.Regt. lands over a Mexeflote. These large pontoons are used for moving heavy vehicles and equipment from ship to shore; each Landing Ship Logistics carries two, and they can be connected to form a floating quay.

Below) Covert reconnaissance is one of the Commandos' specialities; here a patrol in a woodland hide report back using a MEROD Encoder and PRC319 HF/UHF radio.

ship sabotage, and maritime counter-terrorist techniques. Only some 30% of volunteers complete the rigorous selection training for this force of expert swimmers, canoeists, divers and parachutists. Their other skills include navigation, small craft work, demolitions, long range communications and photography. Although their operational work is unceasing it is carried out with a very low profile, and details of SBS organisation and missions remain highly classified - at the time of writing the squadron has been more successful than the Army's SAS in discouraging former members from public indiscretion.

Amphibious Trials & Training Unit RM Responsible for research and development, trials and specialist training in connection with small craft, amphibians, vehicles and plant relevant to the Royal Marines' war roles. Based at Instow on the Bristol Channel, ATTURM is well placed for experimental work in a variety of ocean, estuary and beach environments. The Workshops Team maintains a varied fleet of craft and vehicles including 3x Beach Armoured Recovery Vehicles, 6x trials and training landing craft, various heavy plant and trials vehicles, and even four of the venerable World War II DUKWs - the only true amphibian still in service.

Royal Marines Poole The Specialist Training Unit based at Poole, Dorset houses Landing Craft Wing; Joint Warfare Staff; 148 (Meiktila) Cdo.Bty. RA; Commando Display Team; and HQ Special Boat Squadron.

Commachio Group See page 56.

Royal Marines Reserve A volunteer force with a strength of around 1,220 all ranks. Their roles include bringing units of 3 Cdo.Bde. up to wartime strength, replacement of casualties, and providing certain specialists, watchkeepers and liaison officers.

Royal Marines Band Service

17

(Right) The loads carried by these men of 42 Cdo. during a beach landing underline the absolute necessity for peak physical fitness and stamina. Like airborne troops, Marines making an assault landing may be unsupported and unsupplied for at least three days: if you're going to need it, you carry it - and you may have to carry it a long way.

(Below) Marine deployed in woodland, his L24A1 rifle fitted here with a Kite x4 magnification high performance night sight, which allows accuracy out to 600 yards.

(Opposite) In miserably wet weather - an everyday matter for Marines - men of 42 Cdo. are briefed before a woodland exercise. This man wears a first issue Goretex "breathing" waterproof suit; his weapon is identified by its folded bipod as his fire team's L86A1 Light Support Weapon.

(Above) 42 Commando wait on a forest road for the order to move up during Exercise Purple Warrior; they are equipped for several days and nights in the field. Helmets are naturally issued to Commandos, as to all British servicemen; but it is a matter of pride for Marines (as for their great rivals, the Paras) to honour their WWII traditions by going into action wearing their prized berets. In a "shooting war" such recklessness is - of course - forbidden; and the order is - of course - sometimes disobeyed.

(Right, & opposite bottom left) Combat Net Radio provides communications between the elements of a unit in HF, VHF and UHF bands. The in-service Clansman series is due for replacement by the Bowman.

(Opposite top) The standard personal weapon of the British infantryman is the L24A1 rifle, 5.56mm calibre, fitted as standard with the excellent SUSAT x4 sight which both magnifies and improves marginal light conditions. This rifle and sight combination gives first-round accuracy of better than 96% at 300m, and a soldier really has to try hard not to be a marksman. It takes 30-round magazines, and can fire either semi- or fully automatic.

(Opposite, far right) An LSW gunner of 42 Cdo. cleans his weapon during a brief forest halt. The longer, heavier-barrelled LSW has some 80% commonality of parts with the standard rifle, and takes the same magazines. Its greater muzzle velocity makes the LSW accurate to 800 metres.

(**Left & below**) After landing from a Rigid Raider, Marines in full regulation combat kit use their heavily loaded bergens as rudimentary cover before leaving the open beach.

(**Opposite**) As the assault goes in the Mortar Troop of the Support Coy. start serving their 81mm tubes. The consumption of ammunition by the support weapons of any self-reliant unit like a Commando is staggering, and demands constant resupply by the "Loggies".

GLOBAL COMMANDOS

While the primary mission for which 3 Cdo.Bde. is trained and equipped remains cold weather warfare on NATO's mountainous, arctic northern flank, the strategic role of the Royal Marines demands regular training for several very different environments.

(Above) A Commando photographed during a deployment to Kuwait. (Photo Royal Marines)

(Left) The Mountain & Arctic Warfare Cadre, descended from the old Commando Cliff Assault Wing, provides an elite of highly qualified instructors in climbing, winter survival, and reconnaissance skills, particularly for the recce troops of the Commando units. Entrants must pass the demanding Mountain Leader 3 (ML3) course; and after a tour they are usually drafted to a Commando Recce Troop. In the Falklands War the M&AW Cadre distinguished itself as a 3 Cdo.Bde.HQ intelligence and recce asset. The men of recce sub-units enjoy a good deal of latitude in the matter of preferred kit, such as this popular chest webbing rig.

(Opposite, top & bottom) Although not committed to combat during the Gulf War as formed units, the Commandos played an important part in the subsequent operations in 1991 to set up and protect safe havens for fleeing Kurdish populations in the mountains of northern Iraq. Here a "Jungly" - Marine slang for a Royal Navy HC.4 Sea King helicopter of one of the Naval Air Commando Squadrons - is waved into an LZ, and Commandos deploy.

"CURRY TRAIL"

These annual exercises to maintain levels of jungle training see a composite company, with its own instructing staff, flown out to Brunei. Intensive training in jungle navigation and survival, and the particular challenges of infantry fighting in this environment, culminates in an exercise with the Gurkha Rifles of the permanent garrison. Commandos saw action in the Malayan jungle against Communist terrorists during the "Emergency" of the 1950s and in Borneo against the Indonesian army during the "Confrontation" of the 1960s.

(Left) An exercise umpire watches and makes notes as Marines of 40 Commando treat a simulated casualty.

(Right) RM Commandos, as well as Army infantry battalions, still rotate through Belize, Central America. From the 1960s a British garrison had to deter a long-standing threat against this former British colony from neighbouring Guatemala; this has receded in recent years, but Belize still provides a useful opportunity for jungle training. The waterways offer the only relatively easy routes through the dense forest; consequently they also demand maximum alertness against ambush.

(Below left) A Commando constructs a jungle basha for an overnight halt out of available materials. When complete it will both provide camouflage, and get him and his kit off the jungle floor while he sleeps.

(Below) An RM patrol enter an Indian village up-country in Belize. In tropical environments the Commandos have often carried the US M16A2 rifle and M203 40mm grenade launcher attachment.

(Right & below) The relentless heat and humidity of the Brunei jungle is - according to Commandos familiar with both - more exhausting than the cold of the arctic. The sights, sounds and smells are also claustrophibic and disorienting; an important aim of the training is to instil the confidence which comes only with practice, so that the jungle becomes just one more type of terrain to be harnessed to the advantage of the fighting man.

(Above) Amid a glittering forest
of high-rise buildings, a Gemini
fast inflatable craft of No.3
Raiding Sqn. speeds out of the
harbour of HMS *Tamar*, the
Royal Navy's base in Hong
Kong, before the final hand-over
to the People's Republic in 1997.
Royal Marines carried out regular
waterway patrols against drug
traffickers.

(**Right**) A world away from the
sticky heat of Asia: a gentle
climb on British sea cliffs, with
light kit and in good weather,
would be classed as sheer
recreation by these men of the
Mountain & Actic Warfare
Cadre.

31

SHIP TO SHORE

aval strategy places a high
mphasis on the capability to
operate in any coastal area in the
orld. The inherent flexibility of
ie Royal Marines and the
mphibious Task Group doctrine
nd themselves to these kinds of
perations. The ATG usually
onsists of three elements:
pecialist amphibious shipping,
upporting naval forces, and the
nd force. The former are
presented by:
anding Platform Docks (LPDs)
he two assault ships HMS
earless and *Intrepid* (11,580
ons). Each carries 4x Landing
raft Utility (LCUs) in an
itegral dock with stern access,
x Landing Craft Vehicles &
ersonnel (LCVPs) on davits,
vo support helicopters, and an
nbarked force of 550-700 men.
anding Ships Logistics (LSLs)
here are at present five LSLs
perated by the Royal Fleet
uxiliary, of about 5,600 tons
isplacement. Each can carry
oout 70 vehicles and trailers or
oout 500 troops; they have stern

and bow off-load ramps, their
shallow draught enabling them to
run close inshore, and can also
operate helicopters. The assault
consists of four phases: (1)
Advance forces, in conjunction
with 3 Cdo. Bde. pre-assault
forces (e.g. SBS, Bde. Patrol
Troop) deploy to recce key areas.
(2) Forward Observation teams
also land in order to direct naval
gunfire support for suppression
of enemy activity, and to create
diversions to conceal landing
area.
(3) Mine countermeasures vessels
clear channels to actual and
diversionary landing areas.
(4) The assault begins with the
lifting of two company groups
ashore by landing craft, raiding
craft and hovercraft.

(Left & right) The 13-metre
LCVP has a speed of 14 knots
and a range of 150 nautical
miles.

(Above) A Rigid Raider races
past an LCVP.

(Above) The LCVP can carry a full troop - platoon - of 28 Royal Marines, or an All Terrain Vehicle (ATV), or a Land Rover and trailer.

(Right) An LCU drops its ramp to offload Land Rovers from 40 Commando. The landing craft of 4 & 6 Assault Sqns.RM are permanently based on the LPDs HMS *Fearless* & *Intrepid* respectively, each with four LCVPs and four LCUs; these provide the majority of the craft for the initial off-load.

(Right) Eager Beaver multi-purpose vehicle of the Commando Logistics Rgt. unrolls 11-foot trackway over the beach for the heavy vehicles which will follow. For a large scale operation such as the landing in the Falklands in May 1982 the majority of the follow-up vehicles and stores would be carried on temporarily hired-in merchant ships (STUFT - "ships taken up from trade") including Ro-Ro vehicle ferries.

(Left) Marine Rigid Raiders approach Mexeflotes rigged to the open stern ramp of the RFA *Sir Tristram*, built to replace the LSL of the same name lost at Fitzroy on 8 June 1982 during the most damaging Argentine air attack of the Falklands War.

Left & below) Part of 539 Assault Sqn.'s assets are their four Griffon LCAC(L) hovercraft (Landing Craft Air Cushion Light). The hovercraft can carry 16 troops or 2 tons of stores; they have a top speed of 30 knots, an endurance of 12 hours, and give the Marines flexible mobility over the open sea, beaches, inland waterways, swamps and other restricted areas.

AIR SUPPORT

(Right) As a lightly equipped rapid reaction brigade 3 Cdo.Bde. is trained to operate in conjunction with necessary heavy support elements of the Royal Navy, the Army and the Royal Air Force. Heavy lift for all the services is provided by the RAF's Chinook helicopters, which can carry at least 39 fully equipped troops (and far more in emergencies), or two Land Rovers or ATVs as underslung loads.

(Below) Part of the Commandos' dedicated air support is provided by Nos.845 and 846 Naval Air Commando Squadrons based at RNAS Yeovilton. Here a Sea King HC.4 "Jungly" in desert paintwork hovers as a man is winched up. Each NACS has ten Sea Kings; each can lift 16 Marines and their kit, or an underslung 105mm Light Gun, Land Rover or decoupled ATV. The Sea King is due for replacement by the EH101 Merlin early in the next century. (Photo Westland Helicopters)

Above left) RAF Harrier GR.7s can provide night attack and limited all-weather close air support for the brigade. 1997 saw the first operational deployment of the GR.7 aboard an *Invincible* class carrier. British and Allied air assets can be called in by Tactical Air Control Parties ashore equipped with laser target markers.

Left) The world's only battle-proven Vertical/ Short Take-off & Landing jet fighter bomber, the Harrier is a perfect air support asset for amphibious forces, able to take off fully loaded from short decks and to land vertically. It can be transported on, and flown off from, merchant ships with strengthened decks; and can operate from rough beachhead landing grounds which are quick to prepare. This is the latest mark of the naval version, Sea Harrier F/A-2. Although sub-sonic, the Sea Harrier CAPs protecting the Falklands landings in 1982 accounted for at least 20 Argentine combat jets in air battles. The flexibility of the weapons system represented by the Royal Navy's Sea Harriers and *Invincible* class carriers goes further: at need, one of the three warships in the class can be converted for short term use as a Commando carrier, with 800 Marines and 12 support helicopters embarked. (Photos British Aerospace)

(Above) Sea King HC.4 in arctic garb, and a Lynx AH.7 attack helicopter lifting away, during deployment to IFOR in Bosnia. (Photo Westland Helicopters)

(Right) The brigade cannot be certain of getting suitable vehicles ashore at the right time and place under war conditions; the HC.2 Sea King's lift capacity is vital for getting the guns, men and ammunition of the Commando artillery where and when they are needed in the early stage of a landing operation.

(Far left & left) Another useful trick. . .A Sea King HC.2 lifts a Rigid Raider of 539 Assault Sqn. and its coxswain.

(Below left) No.847 NACS operates six of these TOW-armed Lynx AH.7s, which give the brigade its primary anti-tank capacity; and eight Gazelles for recce, casevac, airborne command posts and general liaison. Both are due to be replaced soon with an up-dated Naval Lynx in the Light Battlefield Helicopter role; and when the Longbow Apache reaches service a "Marinised" Army Air Corps squadron will be embarked, greatly increasing the brigade's aerial firepower.

(Above) Sea King HC.2 lifting off the LPD HMS *Fearless*. The Royal Navy has been pressing for the replacement of the two now-elderly LPDs for some years. The new HMS *Ocean*, an LPH or Commando carrier similar to the 20,000 ton *Invincible* class, was launched in 1995 and is due in service before the end of the century. *Ocean* will carry an embarked force of 800 men, 40 vehicles, four Mk.5 LCVPs and six battlefield helicopters, while also providing a platform for RN Sea Harrier and RAF Harrier GR.7 jets.

NORTHERN EXPOSURE

A stick of Commandos from the Mountain & Arctic Warfare Cadre huddle under the downwash as the Sea King lifts away, leaving them to their own devices in the snowy wastes of northern Norway.

Right) The heavily loaded bergen rucksack, complete with L24A1 rifle camouflaged with white tape.

Below) As daylight fades into the arctic dusk and the temperature drops even further, the party set off across the Hardanger Vidda. "First you are trained to survive in these conditions; then you are trained to fight in them." A nighttime excursion across these frozen wastes tests strength, skills and initiative to the limit.

Although all RM Commandos are trained to operate in the grim conditions of AFNORTH's potential battlefield - where since 1970 the Corps has taken large numbers of Marines for three months of intensive instruction each winter - necessary skills are naturally honed to the highest level by those assets which are tasked with deep reconnaissance in small parties: the M&AW Cadre, Brigade Patrol Troop, and Forward Observation Battery. Their mix of equipment is pragmatically selected; the M16A2/M203 series of US weapons are carried alongside the L24A1. Note chest webbing rigs camouflaged with paint, light nylon snow suits and pack covers (from which snow brushes off easily before it can soak in), and face masks to cut down the massive wind chill encountered in this region.

(Left) Deep inside "bad guys' territory", the shadow under the flank of a snowbank proves on closer inspection to be inhabited by the most dangerous animal on earth.

Patrols may be out for as long as ten days. The recce Commando must learn the arts of digging a snow hole; of cooking his rations on a small napthalene stove (paraffin turns to jelly in these temperatures); and most importantly, of avoiding dehydration. Specially prepared ration packs include such items as chocolate and beef stock drinks, chicken supreme, nuts and raisins.

(Right) The view from inside the well camouflaged covert patrol hide. The visible equipment includes the MEROD encoder, PRC319 HF/UHF secure radio, and the ever-useful image intensifiers for low light vision.

(Below right) Far from base, the isolated patrol can only survive, let alone achieve their mission, by the teamwork which is drummed into every Marine from his first days as a "Noddy". In the arctic environment a buddy system is obviously vital when roping up to climb an ice wall; less dramatic but just as important is the Commandos' care to check each other regularly for the first signs of frostbite.

It is reported that in 1982 a veteran Norwegian officer - with service stretching back to 1940, and personal experience of French, Soviet, German and Austrian mountain troops - declared the Royal Marines to be the best such troops he had seen.

(Above) A patrol member adopts a covering posture at a moment of unavoidable exposure - "popping smoke" to guide in a resupply air drop.

(Right) Marine of the Brigade Patrol Troop about to jump into an arctic DZ from an RAF C-130 Hercules, burdened by main and reserve parachutes, life preserver, and his kit in a CSPEP - Carrying Straps, Personal Equipment, Parachutist. This is a wrapping sheet with an arrangement of quick-release straps, in which the man's bergen and web kit are parcelled up for the drop.

(Opposite top & bottom) Before amphibious landings, pre-assault teams are deployed by various means including parachute insertion. Here a six-man team from the Brigade Patrol Troop shuffle toward the open ramp of a C-130 under the watchful eye of an RAF PJI hooked onto a "loadie's harness". The parachutes are the GQ SSL rig (Static Steerable Line).

Out into the breath-stopping
blast of the arctic slipstream -
check the canopy - check below -
then spring the hooks securing
the CSPEP, and let it fall to the
end of its 5-metre rope tethered
to the leg strap. On snow-covered
DZs the pack's impact with the
ground is a particularly necessary
warning of imminent landing.
The canopy must be collapsed at
once to prevent dragging; then
chute and kit are gathered up.
Every moment spent on the DZ
potentially increases your
vulnerability.

(Left) "Snow wagon" - the Swedish BV.202 tracked all-terrain vehicle - towing skiers of the Brigade Patrol Troop.

(Below) The latest model ATV, the larger Hagglund BV.206. ATVs are available to all the Commandos, providing versatile transport for heavy support weapons and stores. In the future a lightly armoured version is due to be delivered in large numbers.

SNIPERS

It is largely due to the RM Commandos that the special skills of the military sniper - those required apart from a necessarily outstanding level of marksmanship - were maintained in the British armed forces in the decades following World War II. Experience in Northern Ireland at the beginning of the 1970s prompted the Army to seek RM advice on sniper training. The ML2 sniper course at CTC Lympstone lasts five weeks; this is one of the SQs - specialist qualifications - which the recruit may choose after qualifying for his green beret.

These photos show a very basic level of camouflage; by the end of this phase the sniper will have been taught how to fashion for himself an all-enveloping suit of scrim, enabling him to fade completely into the landscape. The sniper's rifle used operationally for many years was the reliable L42A1, a development of the old Enfield No.4 Mk.1(T); in recent trials the 7.62mm L96 has been selected as the replacement. Each Commando has 16 qualified snipers on strength.

COMMACHIO GROUP

This specialist unit based at Arbroath in Scotland is named after a gallant action by 43 Cdo. in northern Italy in April 1945, in which Cpl.Tom Hunter, a Bren gunner, died winning the Victoria Cross.

Commachio Group are responsible for guarding the UK's independent nuclear deterrent at shore establishments such as the Clyde submarine base and the Coulport armaments depot, and other security related sites. They are also responsible for the protection of British off-shore oil platforms; and for certain other duties involving high levels of small boat skills, such as water patrols in Northern Ireland. The Group are maintained on a war footing 365 days a year. High levels of leadership and initiative are demanded by their duties, and selection of volunteers is rigorous and sophisticated.

(Above) A good view of the LSW - the light support weapon variant of the L24A1 rifle, with a longer, heavier barrel for fully automatic fire to longer ranges than the rifle, a metal foregrip and rear pistol grip, and a folding bipod.

(Opposite) Commandos of Commachio Group in an Inflatable Raiding Craft of 539 Assault Sqn.RM. The squadron has 2x LCUs, 4x LCVPs, 4x LCACs, 16x RRCs (Rigid Raiders) and 18x IRCs.

(This page) Commacchio Group Marines storm aboard a "hijacked" vessel from IRCs during an anti-terrorist exercise.

(Opposite) Rigid Raider of 539 ASRM airborne above the waves as it approaches a target at 25 knots; and an RRC coxswain of the squadron. The 8 metre Rigid Raider can carry eight fully equipped Commandos and has a range of 80 nautical miles. The RRC Mk.2 currently in service is due soon for replacement by the Mk.3, with an inboard diesel engine, greater range and higher speed.

(OVERLEAF)
A dusk raid on the Norwegian coast in winter - one of the less comfortable ways to go into battle, on one of the less cheerful battlefields the world has to offer. When operating together with 4 and 6 ASRMs from the *Fearless* and *Intrepid*, 539 ASRM increases the size and flexibility of the brigade's mix of landing craft assets.

(Left) Seen through the eery green eye of an image intensifier, Commandos carry out a night beach assault in Norway. Emphasis has been placed on night combat training throughout the British forces for many years.

(Below & right) Royal Marines divers are tasked with pre-assault recce; they may be inserted by small craft, submarine, helicopter - by a technique known as "heli-casting" - or by parachute. Here they meet an assault party from Commachio Group in the freezing waters of Inverary harbour, Scotland.